GW00866720

Pet Rabbits

Written by
Cath Jones

Rabbits can be good pets.

You can get them in a pet shop.

You can pick rabbits up, but they are not too keen on this.

Pet rabbits need shelter.

If it is hot in the summer,
the hot sunlight can be
too much for them.

They might not feel cool
in such a thick fur coat!

Be sure to keep
the rabbits cool.

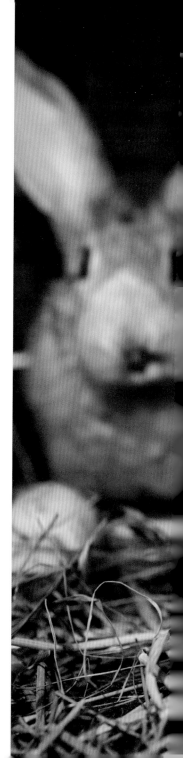

Rabbits need room to run.

A long run in the garden is good for them. It keeps the rabbits fit.

Feed rabbits well.

You can get the right food in a pet shop.

You can feed them carrots and corn too.

A rabbit needs a dish for its food. It might feed at night.

Yum, yum, yum!

A rabbit's tail is short.

It is a 'bob' tail.

This is a Lop Rabbit.
The ears are long and hang down.

Lop Rabbits can hear
well with such long ears.

Long ears keep them cool too.

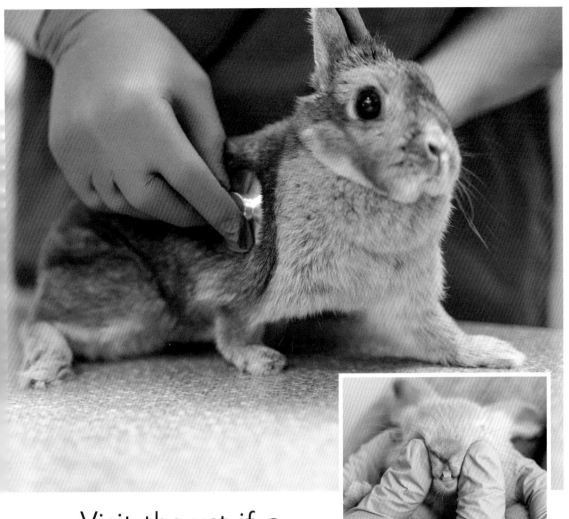

Visit the vet if a
rabbit is unwell or in pain.

The vet can check a rabbit's teeth
too. Teeth can get too long.

This is not a rabbit!